A WREATH FOR
Emmett Till

A WREATH FOR Emmett Till

MARILYN NELSON

ILLUSTRATED BY PHILIPPE LARDY

Houghton Mifflin Company
Boston

FOR INNOCENCE MURDERED. FOR INNOCENCE ALIVE. — M.N.

TO ARIANE. — P.L.

Text copyright © 2005 by Marilyn Nelson
Illustrations copyright © 2005 by Philippe Lardy

www.houghtonmifflinbooks.com

The text of this book is set in Concord Nova.
The illustrations are tempera on cardboard.

Library of Congress Cataloging-in-Publication Data
Nelson, Marilyn, 1946–
A wreath for Emmett Till / Marilyn Nelson ; illustrated by Philippe Lardy.
p. cm.
ISBN 0-618-39752-3
1. Till, Emmett, 1941–1955–Juvenile poetry. 2. African Americans–Crimes against–Juvenile poetry. 3.
African American teenage boys–Juvenile poetry. 4. Trials (Murder)–Juvenile poetry. 5. Murder victims–Juvenile poetry.
6. Hate crimes–Juvenile poetry. 7. Mississippi–Juvenile poetry. 8. Lynching–Juvenile poetry.
9. Children's poetry, American. I. Lardy, Philippe. II. Title.
PS3573.A4795W73 2005
811'.54–dc22
2004009205

ISBN-13: 978-0618-39752-5

Printed in Singapore
TWP 10 9 8 7 6 5 4 3 2

How I Came to Write This Poem

I was nine years old when Emmett Till was lynched in 1955. His name and history have been a part of most of my life. When I decided to write a poem about lynching for young people, I knew that I would write about Emmett Till. He was lynched when he was the age of the young people who might read my poem. After revisiting what I knew about lynching, reading more about it, and growing increasingly depressed, I also knew that I would write this poem as a heroic crown of sonnets.

A sonnet is a fourteen-line rhyming poem in iambic pentameter. The rhyme scheme I chose to use in these sonnets is called Italian, or Petrarchan (after Petrarch, 1304–1374, the poet who invented it). A crown of sonnets is a sequence of interlinked sonnets in which the last line of one becomes the first line, sometimes slightly altered, of the next. A heroic crown of sonnets is a sequence of fifteen interlinked sonnets, in which the last one is made up of the first lines of the preceding fourteen.

When I decided to use this form, I had seen only one heroic crown of sonnets, a fantastically beautiful poem by the Danish poet Inger Christensen. Instead of thinking too much about the painful subject of lynching, I thought about what Inger Christensen's strategy must have been. The strict form became a kind of insulation, a way of protecting myself from the intense pain of the subject matter, and a way to allow the Muse to determine what the poem would say. I wrote this poem with my heart in my mouth and tears in my eyes, breathless with anticipation and surprise.

A Wreath for Emmett Till

R.I.P. Emmett Louis Till, 1941–1955

Rosemary for remembrance, Shakespeare wrote:

a speech for poor Ophelia, who went mad
when her love killed her father. Flowers had
a language then. Rose petals in a note
said, *I love you;* a sheaf of bearded oat
said, *Your music enchants me.* Goldenrod:
Be careful. Weeping-willow twigs: *I'm sad.*
What should my wreath for Emmett Till denote?
First, heliotrope, for *Justice shall be done.*
Daisies and white lilacs, for *Innocence.*
Then mandrake: *Horror* (wearing a white hood,
or bare-faced, laughing). For grief, more than one,
for one is not enough: rue, yew, cypress.
Forget-me-nots. Though if I could, I would

Forget him not. Though if I could, I would

forget much of that racial memory.
No: I remember, like a haunted tree
set off from other trees in the wildwood
by one bare bough. If trees could speak, it could
describe, in words beyond words, make us see
the strange fruit that still ghosts its reverie,
misty companion of its solitude.
Dendrochronology could give its age
in centuries, by counting annual rings:
seasons of drought and rain. But one night, blood,
spilled at its roots, blighted its foliage.
Pith outward, it has been slowly dying,
pierced by the screams of a shortened childhood.

Pierced by the screams of a shortened childhood,

my heartwood has been scarred for fifty years
by what I heard, with hundreds of green ears.
That jackal laughter. Two hundred years I stood
listening to small struggles to find food,
to the songs of creature life, which disappears
and comes again, to the music of the spheres.
Two hundred years of deaths I understood.
Then slaughter axed one quiet summer night,
shivering the deep silence of the stars.
A running boy, five men in close pursuit.
One dark, five pale faces in the moonlight.
Noise, silence, back-slaps. One match, five cigars.
Emmett Till's name still catches in the throat.

Emmett Till's name still catches in my throat,

like syllables waylaid in a stutterer's mouth.
A fourteen-year-old stutterer, in the South
to visit relatives and to be taught
the family's ways. His mother had finally bought
that White Sox cap; she'd made him swear an oath
to be careful around white folks. She'd told him the truth
of many a Mississippi anecdote:
Some white folks have blind souls. In his suitcase
she'd packed dungarees, T-shirts, underwear,
and comic books. She'd given him a note
for the conductor, waved to his chubby face,
wondered if he'd remember to brush his hair.
Her only child. A body left to bloat.

Your only child, a body thrown to bloat,

mother of sorrows, of justice denied.
Surely you must have thought of suicide,
seeing his gray flesh, chains around his throat.
Surely you didn't know you would devote
the rest of your changed life to dignified
public remembrance of how Emmett died,
innocence slaughtered by the hands of hate.
If sudden loving light proclaimed you blest
would you bow your head in humility,
your healed heart overflow with gratitude?
Would you say yes, like the mother of Christ?
Or would you say no to your destiny,
mother of a boy martyr, if you could?

Mutilated boy martyr, if I could,

I'd put you in a parallel universe,
give you a better fate. There is none worse.
I'd let you live through a happy boyhood,
let your gifts bloom into a livelihood
on a planet that didn't bear Cain's curse.
I'd put you in a nice, safe universe,
not like this one. A universe where you'd
surpass your mother's dreams. But parallel
realities may have terrorists, too.
Evil multiplies to infinitude,
like mirrors facing each other in hell.
You were a wormhole history passed through,
transformed by the memory of your victimhood.

Erase the memory of Emmett's victimhood.

Let's write the obituary of a life
lived well and wisely, mourned by a loving wife
or partner, friends, and a vast multitude.
Remember the high purpose he pursued.
Remember how he earned a nation's grief.
Remember accomplishments beyond belief,
honors enough to make us ooh, slack-jawed,
as if we looked up at a meteor shower
or were children watching a fireworks display.
Let America remember what he taught.
Or at least let him die in a World Trade tower
rescuing others, that unforgettable day,
that memory of monsters, that bleak thought.

The memory of monsters: That bleak thought

should be confined to a horror-movie world.
A horror classic, in which a blind girl
hears, one by one, the windows broken out,
an ax at the front door. In the onslaught
of terror, as a hate-filled body hurls
itself against her door, her senses swirl
around one prayer: Please, God, forget me not.
The body-snatchers jiggle the doorknob,
werewolves and vampires slaver after blood,
the circus of nightmares is here. She screams,
he screams, neighbors with names he knows, a mob
heartless and heedless, answering to no god,
tears through the patchwork drapery of our dreams.

Tears, through the patchwork drapery of dream,

for the hanging bodies, the men on flaming pyres,
the crowds standing around like devil choirs,
the children's eyes lit by the fire's gleams
filled with the delight of licking ice cream,
men who hear hog screams as a man expires,
watch-fob good-luck charms teeth pulled out with pliers,
sinners I can't believe Christ's death redeems,
your ash hair, Shulamith–Emmett, your eye,
machetes, piles of shoes, bulldozed mass graves,
the broken towers, the air filled with last breaths,
the blasphemies pronounced to justify
the profane, obscene theft of human lives.
Let me gather spring flowers for a wreath.

Let me gather spring flowers for a wreath.

Not lilacs from the dooryard, but wildflowers
I'd search for in the greening woods for hours
of solitude, meditating on death.
Let me wander through pathless woods, beneath
the choirs of small birds trumpeting their powers
at the intruder trampling through their bowers,
disturbing their peace. I cling to the faith
that innocence lives on, that a blind soul
can see again. That miracles do exist.
In my house, there is still something called grace,
which melts ice shards of hate and makes hearts whole.
I bear armloads of flowers home, to twist
into a circle: trillium, Queen Anne's lace . . .

Trillium, apple blossoms, Queen Anne's lace,

woven with oak twigs, for sincerity . . .
Thousands of oak trees around this country
groaned with the weight of men slain for their race,
their murderers acquitted in almost every case.
One night five black men died on the same tree,
with toeless feet, in this Land of the Free.
This country we love has a Janus face:
One mouth speaks with forked tongue, the other reads
the Constitution. My country, 'tis of both
thy nightmare history and thy grand dream,
thy centuries of good and evil deeds,
I sing. Thy fruited plain, thy undergrowth
of mandrake, which flowers white as moonbeams.

Indian pipe, bloodroot. White as moonbeams,

their flowers. Picked, one blackens, and one bleeds
a thick red sap. Indian pipe, a weed
that thrives on rot, is held in disesteem,
though it does have its use in nature's scheme,
unlike the rose. The bloodroot poppy needs
no explanation here: Its red sap pleads
the case for its inclusion in the theme
of a wreath for the memory of Emmett Till.
Though the white poppy means *forgetfulness*,
who could forget, when red sap on a wreath
recalls the brown boy five white monsters killed?
Forgetting would call for consciencelessness.
Like the full moon, which smiled calmly on his death.

Like the full moon, which smiled calmly on his death.

Like the stars, which fluttered their quicksilver wings.

Like the unbroken song creation sings

while humankind tramples the grapes of wrath.

Like wildflowers growing beside the path

a boy was dragged along, blood spattering

their white petals as he, abandoning

all hope, gasped his agonizing last breath.

Like a nation sending its children off to fight

our faceless enemy, immortal fear,

the most feared enemy of the human race.

Like a plague of not knowing wrong from right.

Like the consciencelessness of the atmosphere.

Like a gouged eye, watching boots kick a face.

Like his gouged eye, which watched boots kick his face,

we must bear witness to atrocity.
But we are whole: We can speak what we see.
People may disappear, leaving no trace,
unless we stand before the populace,
orators denouncing the slavery
to fear. For the lynchers feared the lynchee,
what he might do, being of another race,
a great unknown. They feared because they saw
their own inner shadows, their vicious dreams,
the farthest horizons of their own thought,
their jungles immune to the rule of law.
We can speak now, or bear unforgettable shame.
Rosemary for remembrance, Shakespeare wrote.

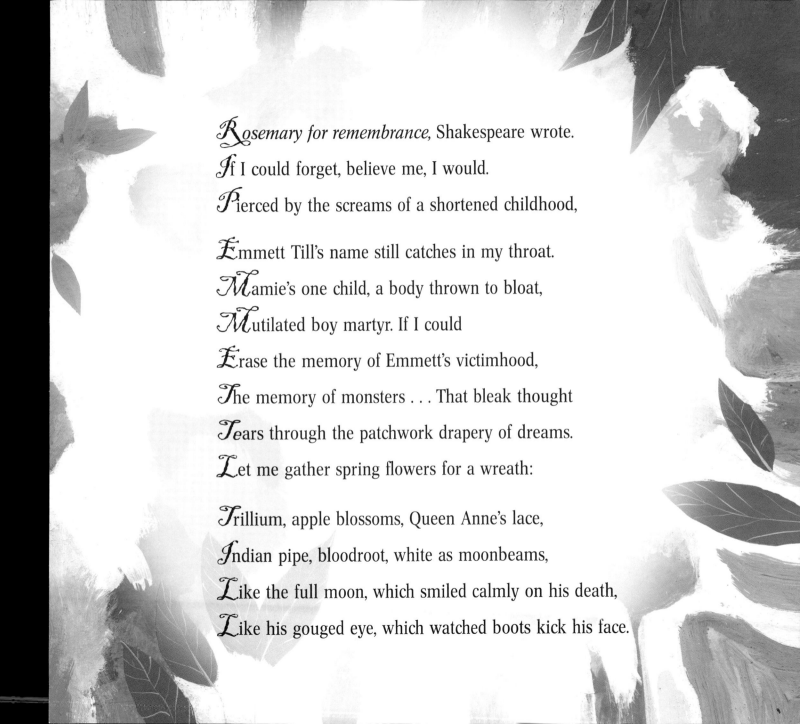

Rosemary for remembrance, Shakespeare wrote.

If I could forget, believe me, I would.

Pierced by the screams of a shortened childhood,

Emmett Till's name still catches in my throat.

Mamie's one child, a body thrown to bloat,

Mutilated boy martyr. If I could

Erase the memory of Emmett's victimhood,

The memory of monsters . . . That bleak thought

Tears through the patchwork drapery of dreams.

Let me gather spring flowers for a wreath:

Trillium, apple blossoms, Queen Anne's lace,

Indian pipe, bloodroot, white as moonbeams,

Like the full moon, which smiled calmly on his death,

Like his gouged eye, which watched boots kick his face.

Who was Emmett Till?

Emmett Louis Till was born in Chicago on July 25, 1941. He was a friendly, extroverted African American boy who grew up during a time when racism and segregation were legal parts of the culture of the United States.

In the summer of 1955, fourteen-year-old Emmett visited relatives in the South. On August 24, in the town of Money, Mississippi, Emmett went into a country store, where, by some accounts, he whistled at a white woman. On August 28, the woman's husband and brother-in-law took Emmett from his uncle's house. Emmett's body was found three days later. The murderers had tied a heavy metal cotton gin fan to his neck with barbed wire and thrown him into the Tallahatchie River. He had been shot in the head. His face and body had been beaten and were bloated from the river water.

Emmett's mother, Mamie Till Mobley, held an open-casket funeral in Chicago to show what had been done to her son. Thousands of people stood in line for the viewing. Graphic photos appeared in newspapers and magazines, galvanizing anger across the nation.

An all-white male jury heard the trial of the alleged murderers in a segregated courthouse in Mississippi. In spite of the terrors of the times and the danger he could have been placing himself in, Emmett's uncle identified the white men who had pulled Emmett out of his house. After deliberating for just over an hour, the jurors came back with a verdict of not guilty. The trial and verdict drew the world's attention.

People around the country–both black and white–who previously had felt separated from southern racism were shocked by Emmett Till's death and outraged by the injustice of his killers' trial. The lynching of the boy Emmett Till helped spark the civil rights movement of the late 1950s and 1960s.

Months after the trial, one of the former defendants told a reporter how they had killed Emmett. Years later, the two men tried for Emmett's murder said that three others were involved.

Sonnet Notes

I.

This sonnet alludes to act iv, scene v of Shakespeare's *Hamlet*, when Ophelia, driven mad by grief for her murdered father, says, "There's rosemary, that's for remembrance; pray, love, remember: and there is pansies. That's for thoughts." The idea of a language of flowers is an ancient tradition.

II.

This sonnet alludes first to an earlier poem, "The Haunted Oak," by Paul Laurence Dunbar. In Dunbar's poem, an oak tree describes a lynching. The second allusion is to "Strange Fruit," a poem about lynching written by Lewis Allen and made famous as a song by the great blues singer Billie Holiday. Dendrochronology is the science of telling a tree's age by counting the rings in its trunk.

III.

In this sonnet the tree speaks, describing its long life of witnessing natural deaths and killings, and the one unnatural killing, which was so horrible that it made part of the tree die.

IV.

This sonnet takes us back to the human voice of the poet. Emmett Till was a stutterer; his mother had encouraged him to whistle when he could not get a word out. He was lynched because a white woman in Money, Mississippi, said he had whistled at her.

The White Sox were one of the two major league baseball teams based in Chicago in the 1950s. Because the White Sox home field was on the south side of the city, near the area where most of the African-Americans in Chicago lived, most of them were White Sox fans. If Emmett Till was a baseball fan, he would probably have wanted to wear a White Sox cap.

V.

This sonnet compares the pain of Emmett Till's mother, Mamie Till Mobley, to the pain of Mary, the mother of Jesus, who is also known to Christians as "the Mother of Sorrows." Mary was "proclaimed blest" by the angel who came to her at the Annunciation, when she was pregnant, and said, "Hail, Mary, Mother of God. Blessed art thou among women." Mamie Till Mobley insisted that her son should lie in an open casket so the world could see how savagely he had been murdered. His naked body was horribly mangled, his nose severed, his head cleaved nearly in two, one eye gouged out. For the rest of her life, Emmett's mother was an activist for civil rights. She died in 2003 at the age of eighty-one.

VI.

Some scientists now believe that there may be an infinite number of parallel universes and that we just happen to live in one of them. Superstring theory, hyperspace, and dark matter made physicists realize that the three dimensions they had thought described the universe weren't enough. There are actually eleven dimensions. Some physicists now think that our universe may be just one "bubble" among an infinite number of "bubbles" that ripple as they wobble through the eleventh dimension. The universes parallel to ours contain space, time, and matter. Some of them may even contain us, in a slightly different form. Science-fiction writers have enjoyed speculating about what a parallel universe might be like.

The biblical Cain, one of the sons of Adam and Eve, committed the first murder when he killed his brother Abel.

In physics, a wormhole is a tunnel in the geometry of space-time, postulated to connect different parts of the universe or to enable time travel.

VII.

This sonnet considers the lives Emmett Till might have lived in several parallel universes. Would he have grown up to marry and be a father? Would he have been a great man? Would his memory have been mourned and honored? Would he have died on September 11, 2001, saving people from the monsters who caused so many deaths in the World Trade Center?

VIII.

The thought of "monsters" leads to the thought of monster movies, in which we identify with the trapped and powerless victims. The "blind girl" described here alludes to the 1967 film *Wait Until Dark*, which starred Audrey Hepburn as a blind girl trapped in her apartment and terrorized by a psychotic killer. In the poem, the monsters turn out to be the same kind of "monsters" who attacked Emmett Till: ordinary people, neighbors, friends. Mob mentality transforms ordinary thinking and caring people into an entity with no mind, no heart, and no God.

IX.

Awakening from the scary movie, we enter a real-life nightmare, more horrible than a scene from a movie. Late-nineteenth- and early-twentieth-century American lynch mobs often took photographs of their victims, burning heaps of human flesh or hanged naked men, surrounded by grinning crowds. These were sent as postcards to friends and relatives. A recent book, *Without Sanctuary: Lynching Photography in America* (edited by James Allen, Twin Palms Publishers, 2000) includes some eighty of these. The descriptions of lynch mobs in this sonnet are based on that book.

This sonnet is all one sentence, the speed of which accelerates as it lists details of lynchings and other real-life nightmares in which neighbors slaughtered their neighbors. "Machetes" is a hinted reference to the genocidal attacks on Rwanda's Tutsi people by their Hutu neighbors; "piles of shoes" hints at the Nazi gas chambers; "bulldozed mass graves" hints at the genocidal attacks of Serbs on ethnic Albanians in the land once known as Yugoslavia.

"The broken towers" alludes to the World Trade Center and to the towers of Troy, the city-state destroyed in the Trojan War.

X.

There are several literary allusions in this sonnet:

"Lilacs from the dooryard" alludes to Walt Whitman's great elegy for Abraham Lincoln, "When Lilacs Last in the Dooryard Bloomed."

"Pathless woods" alludes to Robert Frost's poem "Birches."

"Choirs of small birds" alludes to Shakespeare's sonnet #73.

"In my house there is still" alludes to a speech by the mother in Lorraine Hansberry's 1959 play *A Raisin in the Sun.*

"Ice shards of hate" alludes to Hans Christian Andersen's fairy tale "The Snow Queen."

XI.

Janus, the Roman god of beginnings and endings and of gates, lent his name to the month of January. He was depicted with two faces looking in opposite directions, both forward and backward.

"Speaks with forked tongue" alludes to a Native American saying about the whites who made treaties with tribes, then broke them.

XII.

"Consciencelessness," or lacking a conscience, in this sonnet describes the simple innocence of the natural world, which transcends human morality.

XIII.

This sonnet continues the description of the "consciencelessness" of the natural world, but then leaps to consider how and when the human world displays similar "consciencelessness." It suggests this happens when a nation forgets right and wrong and tries to wage war against fear itself. The sonnet alludes to President Franklin D. Roosevelt's 1933 inauguration speech in which he said, "The only thing we have to fear is fear itself."

XIV.

"Orators denouncing the slavery/to fear" alludes to the abolitionists (including William Lloyd Garrison, Frederick Douglass, Sojourner Truth, Wendell Phillips, and Susan B. Anthony) of the middle nineteenth century, who risked their reputations, their safety, and their lives by speaking out against slavery.

XV.

This last sonnet is composed of the first lines from the preceding fourteen sonnets.

ARTIST'S NOTE

This poem is structured much like a painting. It has symbols, layers, colors, geometry, and even a sense of space. I have tried to translate these elements into paint and to render the poem's rhythm through a succession of small and large images. My approach was to emphasize the contrast between the delicate and decorative natural elements, such as flowers, with the sheer horror of the crime. I divided the poem into three parts, demarcated by "interludes" of green, a calm and remote color.

I named the first part "the crime." Using the color red, I painted a tree cut in half to symbolize Emmett Till's suffering. I did not want to be too literal here, showing his actual body, since I felt a symbol would be more thought-provoking. For me, the tree becomes both the place of Emmett's execution and the symbol of his corpse. On the tree stump, the mandrake plant, with its anthropomorphic shape, is a metaphor for Emmett's victimhood (traditionally, the mandrake was depicted as growing under gallows).

The crows surrounding the scene have a double meaning. For nineteenth-century Romantic poets, crows represented death and had a strong negative connotation. In this sense, the crows are Emmett Till's murderers. But in many civilizations, such as the Native Americans and the Egyptians, crows are a positive image. In ancient Egypt, the crow led the soul on its journey from life to death. In that sense, the birds serve as guides.

Emmett's face is surrounded by a wreath of wires, chains, and thorns. This depicts the means of his murder, but is also a biblical reference to Jesus' crown and martyrdom.

I used the elliptic shape to unite the elements of the first part, alluding to the wreath's shape; the stage on which the action takes place; and the "cosmic egg," the mythological origin of the universe.

I call the second part "the mourning." In this section, I used earthy mineral colors for loss. The brown background represents earth and death, but also transformation into new life, new meaning.

In contrast to the other parts, the rectangle was used throughout this second section: it is a coffin when placed horizontally, an evocation of the World Trade Center when tilted vertically. Flowers are placed in these dark settings, for hope and transcendence. The double-page spread depicts a number of coffins, one of which holds the image of Emmett Till. This stands as an icon of all anonymous victims.

The third part, what I call "the lesson," uses plenty of orange and yellow–for hope. Ellipses overlap here, fusing black and white within one's own consciousness, reflecting the contrasting forces present in the poem–subtle and brutal, ideal and destructive. *A Wreath For Emmett Till* challenges us to recognize these forces within ourselves, our cultures, our governments, and the way we treat our environment. I have tried to illustrate this challenge and the poem's assurance that by bringing to light the hidden forces behind our actions, we can change the world.

–*Philippe Lardy*

REFERENCES
WEB SITE
The Murder of Emmett Till: www.pbs.org/wgbh/amex/till.
The PBS site feature is a companion to the PBS film about Emmett Till and includes primary sources, stories, a timeline, and a teacher's guide.

BOOKS

Crowe, Chris. *Getting Away with Murder: The True Story of the Emmett Till Case.* New York: Dial, 2003.
Metress, Christopher. *The Lynching of Emmett Till: A Documentary Narrative.* Charlottesville: University of Virginia Press, 2002.
Till-Mobley, Mamie, and Christopher Benson. *Death of Innocence: The Story of the Hate Crime That Changed America.* New York: Random House, 2003.